Edgar Lewis Wakeman

Winter-Freed

A Summer Idyl

Edgar Lewis Wakeman

Winter-Freed
A Summer Idyl

ISBN/EAN: 9783337258412

Printed in Europe, USA, Canada, Australia, Japan

Cover: Foto ©Andreas Hilbeck / pixelio.de

More available books at **www.hansebooks.com**

WINTER-FREED:

A SUMMER IDYL.

BY

EDGAR LEWIS WAKEMAN.

AUTHOR'S EDITION.

CHICAGO:

ADAMS, BLACKMER, & LYON.

1866.

TO

THE THOUSANDS

WHOSE HEARTS BEAT WARM AND FREE

AS THE

TALE OF THEIR YOUTH IS REPEATED,

THIS POEM IS DEDICATED,

BY

THE AUTHOR.

" Like souls that balance joy and pain,

With tears and smiles from heaven again

The maiden Spring upon the plain

Came in a sun-lit fall of rain.

In crystal vapor everywhere

Blue isles of heaven laugh'd between,

And far in forest deeps unseen

The topmost elm tree gathered green

From draughts of balmy air."

TENNYSON.

PRELUDE.

Back, through the deep'ning maze of years,

The mind of Now with one bound clears;

And scene on scene of early joy

Comes — thronging through the strange alloy

Of life; along in pictured truth

They sing the poetry of youth:

The poetry that hurts us not

To think upon and often dote:

That, in the sad, dark things that be,

Comes to us with its ministry, —

Smoothing the jutting edges — oft

Making the weary pillow soft:

PRELUDE.

Pressing down the plaids of strife,

And in each oasis of life

Inserting little streams of pure,

Bright water, always to endure ;

And down whose shaded, grassy brink

The weary pilgrim bends to drink.

WINTER-FREED.

IRED, and full impatient of old
Winter's too long continued cold,
We hailed, with wild and glad delight,
The Spring appearing to our sight.
Glad the joyous summons now,
Of " Boys, down with the spade and plow !"
The winter's rest had giv'n anew
The will to work, and things to do
Were righted quickly — out we went,
Filled with the spring-time merriment.

11

The fields, so autumn-brown and bare,

Were ploughed again with greatest care—

Sowed seed; did all our spring's work up—

Out, where nods the violet's cup,

We drove the cows, that they might taste

Upon the beauteous prairie waste,

And nip the bright green buds, and come

At night with streaming udders home:

Then let them in the barn-yard gate,

Where fretting, weary they must wait

Till we released them of their load.

By sober winks they always showed

They loved the task of giving food;

And when the pails were filled, they stood

A moment watching as we passed,

Then down upon the ground they cast

Their pond'rous forms, and gladly pressed

Their cuds again in happy rest.

WINTER-FREED.

With sleeves uprolled and head all bare,

The cool wind toying with his hair,

Our father on the low porch stands

Complacent, looking on his lands,

His barns, his kine and hard-earned soil,

Or sagely planning morrow's toil.

Ah! years have brought their weary tasks,

Life has assumed its many masks,

Up through each one in sadness come

A fretted minaret and dome

Of hopes and efforts dead and gone,

And wild desire that's with them flown!

But even now, while waiting, I,

Like some lone leaf that's left to die,

And tempest-beaten, dun and brown,

Just stopping a little, till down

By friendly gust in turn shall fall,

And 'neath the oaks so great and tall,

Lie with the rest of withered leaves —

Lie till the great earth madly heaves ; —

Can see him calmly standing now :

And round his weather-beaten brow

The dim, far distance, seems to send

A halo fair, and brightly lend

A golden radiance to the scene,

That's pure and peaceful and serene.

Our pails within the milk-house doors

Concluded all our nightly chores.

Now, out upon the dew-tipped grass,

Before the twilight all should pass,

We rolled and scrambled merrily,

And romped in hurly-burly glee ;

Standing beside our father staid,

And still, and watching as we played ,

With full the knowledge (so we said)

Of grey old Grave-face, justice, 'squire,

And leader of the village choir,

Our house-dog seems to think the sport

Too tame, or something of that sort;

For down he pounces with one bound,

And strews the soft and matted ground

With bodies of our luckless horde,

As we in silent wonder heard

How Samson came from Etam's Rock,

Hearing the loud Philistines' mock,

Then burst his cords, and strewed the plain

With heaps, his jaw-boned thousand, slain.

Soon, breaking up this merry din,

And bidding each of us come in,

Our father's voice was plainly heard:

So, quick into the house we passed;

For early had we learned — and fast,

To do his bidding, at the word.

And now, within the kitchen walls,
The scene grows dim as darkness falls;
Our mother brings the lights, and sits
Musing quietly as she knits.
Mother! that name shall fondly live
Until the ready, waiting grave
Shall take me hence; and even go
To its dark caverns, deep and low,
With all the sacred love that burns
Within the pure and chastened urns
Of deep affection's holy shrine —
Well fed from Love's o'erflowing mine!
O, Time! thy guarded vigils keep;
Thy overflowing harvests reap!
On man, thy unrelenting Change,
Stamp in the stillness of thy strange

And mystic workings ; thy dark, deep,

Grim orgies hold, then quickly leap

And carry out thy ripened plan —

Thy ruin to the heart of man !

Thou, who art the greatest and first

Of robbers, do thy fiercest, worst,

And sink thy barbed arrows deep ;

Sear, as a leaf, man's soul ; and keep

Thy joys in guarded scrutiny ;

Lock thy pleasure-safes ; let there be

No peace to nestle near his heart ;

Steal in upon him, and apart

From Hope's glad fields, make isolate,

And quickly, then, when almost sate

Are thy rapacious jaws, lick up

The life-blood from the shattered cup !

A new found morsel for thy food —

The last and best and greatest good

Which greets thy hungered, maddened sense,

And almost makes thy heart relent —

Is — burning bright and free and pure —

Burning with love-light to endure —

Burning as stars at holy even —

Burning as angel-light in heaven —

Or radiance up there Above, —

A never-dying mother-love !

The oaken table, nicely wrought

By hands love-skilled and wisely taught

In frugal thrift and early lore,

Most practiced in the days of yore,

Was brought: all gathered quickly near,

The weekly news intent to hear:

Or, an eager party, as quite

Out of the feeble candle-light,

We pressed around our grandsire sage —

His form was bent, and certain age

Had bleached his hair a soft, pure white,

Like as the gathered frosts of night, —

To hear, in childish wonderment,

How Continental soldiers sent

From off our shores, in baffled rage,

The hireling British vassalage !

In measured cadence, still and slow,

At first he spake, and, like the low,

Sweet rippling of the meadow-stream —

Gently as talking in a dream ;

Then Time's veil was slowly lifted,

As the low-hung mists are drifted,

Quick-leaving through the clear, pure air,

The mountain's side distinct and bare :

Or, as we see the silv'ry sheen

Of flashing stars, then right between

Where all seemed but the great, deep blue,

We see a wand'rer peeping through:

So he caught the far-off youth-calls;

Low at first, but as the rain falls,

In little patters, few and still,

Then faster, till they hastening fill

The air, and beat in quick and wild

Confusion — gone were his mild looks,

And the spirit that fast stirred

When of our wrongs indignant heard,

Thrilled through his service-beaten frame,

And lightly mocked destroyer Time!

Yes, quick-dropping years may fast

Fall in the calendar of Past;

They may take with them fortune, all

That serves to light the darkened halls

Of life, one legacy they leave:

Our benison they cannot cleave.

Mute it may be, yet not profound

Its sleep; for, at the slightest sound,

Its former fervor may awake,

And, like the pent-up stream, quick break

The dam, time-worn and old, and rush

Through with a wilder, fiercer gush

For its frail and feeble bindings!

Thus thronged by recollections fast,

Proud grew his form; one that had cast

With all the strength that can be giv'n

A noble cause, by righteous heaven,

A weapon, tyrant-feared and strong,

Directed to the heart of Wrong:

Mute hung an empty sleeve; fit proof

His words were true, and that aloof

From danger he had scorned to be.

That empty sleeve! how wild and free

The tale it tells ! and now, when we

Can see the war-clouds give away

And breaking through the beauteous day ;

Can feel our country's pulse beat on,

And throb in mutual unison, —

And hear the glad, exultant shout

A noble nation can ring out,

And see that only arm wave free

With its twice load of liberty,

We say "proud hero !" well thou hast

Won thy laurels which will last.

That empty sleeve, which flutters, fair,

Has room to undulate in air

Made sacred, by the manly heart

That nerved that arm to do its part :

Yes, thou hast won the hallowed right

Of bearing, with thy war-dimmed sight,

A purer, dearer, fitter boon

Than monuments of costly stone:

A holy Mecca dost thou wear;

A nation's heart oft journeys there,

With glist'ning tear-drops, quick to bring

A grateful freeland's offering!

Drinking in each column's news,

Or list'ning to our father's views,

Accepting quick each slender chance

Her store of knowledge to enhance, —

Breaking the rugged, shapeless stone

In fragments, and untaught, alone

Catching gleams of precious light

From dross-wrapt gems, to make more bright

Her clouded, dream-land mysteries,

And sooner dawn upon her eyes

The life-ideal, which had wrought

Such wondrous change in word and thought,

Our sister sat, half-loved, half-feared:

She led another life than we;

And journeyed to immensity

Her ready soul, catching the gleams

Radiated from brighter beams

Of light than we might ever know.

Her eager nature craved and sought

A fairer realm to dream, where naught

Of common circumstance might come

And drive the basking spirit down

The long, steep stairs, whose each descent

Marks where other souls have rent

The charm which buoyed them up, and fell

With naught but world-gain visible.

Such life she led; but never thought

Of scorn for us, who had not caught

The deep-drawn inspiration.   Nor
Felt she ever world-styled proud ; for
The true spirit no stress of voice
Holds on the stations God's choice
Has meted out ! and even now
Her own hand held the strained bow
    Of household duties : well she filled
    Her double mission, and distilled
Around a genial, ruddy glow.

Such hearts are needed, even now,
The growing evils to surmount,
And dash away the fatal fount
Deep-seated Fashion gushes forth,
With all its vice and sin, and dearth
Of goodly fruits, and plant right there
Far different seed, which, by good care,
Might grow and blossom, fair and full

WINTER-FREED.

Of all that's good and beautiful:

Blest circle! now almost complete:
But one, whose weary, wandering feet
Tread the wild paths of life, apart
From the warm, loving, household heart:
A nature impassionate and strange,
Subjected oft to sudden change;
Combining, with a heart of love,
The flash that reason cannot move;
Thus exiled by his own blind will,
Stern chiding was not best to still
His mind inflamed: like as the waves,
Which, pile on pile, leap up and lave
And beat the rocks in maudlin rage,
Need no wild, fierce winds to assuage
Their heaving swell.   No one might tell
How this young heart strove brave and well

WINTER-FREED.

To cultivate the yielding soil
Of life; and, by severest toil,
Bring forth rich fruit, that we might view
The goodly work which he could do.

Our father, often sternly, had
The mentioning of his name forbade;
Yet, frequent was the whispered word
Which told that love yet fondly stirred
Within our bosoms, warm and true,
To him far from our eager view:
And (being like all frail ideals
That man conceives, far distance steals
The faults, and paints more bright
Good qualities brought out to light,)
We saw him as our brother yet —

    As when he left us, kind as then —
His only fault too pure a view

Of honor worn by other men !

Great hearts ! do not condemn unjust :

How many crafts by heaven built well

Draw anchor in a harbor wild,

To seek the ocean's broader swell,

Lest rigging, sails, and towering spars

Wreck on the white, uplooming bars ;

Choosing to fight a fiercer storm,

Than while at anchor feel alarm !

Out from the bright, green fields of youth,

Basking in the sweet light of truth,

How many look across the way,

Catching a little brighter ray

From petals, seeming fairer blown !

Frail hands quick grasp the wall of stone,

And never stop those bleeding feet,

Till almost o'er the false, dark street —

Tired, and sick, and late the hour,

Find other souls have plucked the flower !

The paper's columns closely scanned,

Our father sits with head in hands.

Our mother knits on quietly ;

Our sister, lost in reverie,

Journeys to that great Unknown

Whose boundless shores she feels her own !

And we, around our grandsire, all

Felt the ominous silence fall.

The clock, against the hard oak wall,

Sounded its pendulum voice in thrall ;

And thus, in measured, meaning beat,

Told that " time flies," and all must meet !

Perhaps this thought found entrance, where

Fell, in light folds, our mother's hair ;

And fluttered through a father's heart,
As thus he mused the world apart.

Out from the shoreless, great Unknown —
    Out from the rayless shadows, dark, —
Out from the close-drawn horizon's rim,
    Which sternly hides that wand'ring bark,
And makes all deep, dark mystery
Around their roving, banished boy,
Perhaps a gentle spirit drifts —
A tiny craft, whose sail uplifts,
Filled with a zephyr heaven-blown, —
Half-way to fondly meet its own;
And gently toy in the rich mart
Built in every parent's heart:
Perhaps they clasp that spirit-boy:
Clasp the sweet, sinless purity;
Clasp the soft artlessness, the truth,

And smiling innocence of youth.

The silence broken, now we sang

   Our evening hymn; our father's prayer

Came low and soft, and more subdued;

   As though the soul found entrance, where

Its watching angels met to bruit

The knowledge of rich, golden fruit,

Seeding and rip'ning in an hour,

Nourished by God's forgiving power.

He grasped the outstretched hand of Love;

And asked that He who rules Above,

Would watch those feet impassionate;

Would keep aloof from adverse fate;

Would guide, whatever lands they roam;

And if the rugged, jutting stone

Should bruise and tear their tender flesh,

   That He would ease their rough, dark way

Bind up their wounds, break the vile mesh

    That snares, and dawn a fairer day.

Our father closed his earnest prayer;

Each silently sought our rooms, where

We might unnoticed drop a tear, —

Might ask anew that God would hear;

And feel soft peace and quietness

Steal o'er our senses, bringing rest!

Ah! little world, so full of pain,

Sometimes thy sorrows loose their reign!

Sometimes, quick through all thy sad guile,

Bursts the rich bloom, and angels smile!

And thus the farm-house stands to-night,

Resplendent in the soft, pure light;

Nestling 'neath its guardian trees,

Like fairy genii gods at ease.

How like it looks, as there it rests,

To little birds in cosy nests ;

Or the freed hearts within its walls,

In shrouds of love as sweet peace falls :

The little brook, that prattled by,

Has hushed its noisy revelry :

The cooing dove, beneath the eaves,

Its tale of love till morrow leaves ;

The creaking swing of the one-hinged gate

The morning winds in sighing waits,

And where some tall tree's towering crest

Breaks the bright light, aud shadows rest

Deeper — darker, with sombre cast,

Strange shapes form on the glitt'ring grass.

How sweet to view the picture now,

When thorns cling round the weary brow :

When oft the sad heart, sorrow-pressed,

Seeks, yet finds no happy rest:

How cool the balm seems to a torn,

Hurt soul, just now its worth we learn.

We turn the pages later years,

Find each one torn and wet with tears;

Back to the little ones we turn,

Leaving accounts and things more stern,

To see if ever through life's Book,

We may find the pages, which will look

Happy and peaceful, — free from pain;

Shining and pure, and without stain.

Sad, we near where the leaves grow small,

And deep and dark the shadows fall:

The light's most out, yet we can see

Lying there, calm and peacefully,

    Beautiful scenes: though faint and small,

Bright specks on life's horizon cast,

WINTER-FREED.

Urging us back with sweet, low call!
We grasp gems here, and flowers there;
And fill with pearls our time-thinned hair,—
Revel, and pluck of all the best;
Thus distilling beautiful rest!

The morn broke o'er us, gladly fair:
Up from the meadows, came the air
Full laden with bewitching breath,
Gleaned from the hare-bells on the heath!
Gleaned from the clover, where the flocks
Swept o'er the rich fields, giving mock
To winter's stinted, guarded fare,
Cropping the juicy herbage bare!

Now the corn-ploughing time has come;
How the leaves rustle, and talk, and hum,
Prattling their tales of autumn-wealth!

And how the little green ear, in stealth,

Peeps out through the bright, silken hair—

Peeps out and looks 'round everywhere,

Bowing and bending, to catch a glimpse

Of the fairy little lowland nymphs,

Dancing, and holding their orgies, still,

Under the shade of its spreading frill !

How, up to the bright, shining sun,

Turn its broad leaves — turn every one ;

How they glitter and wave, and so

Out to the ploughing quick we go.

We are happy : we always find

Strange intelligence, almost mind,

In these little tokens of the air,

The trees, the birds, — and everywhere

Beautiful summer in rich wealth,

Bringing contentment, joy, and health !

Thus passed the time: the long week's work

Then Sabbath, blessed day of rest,

When God was worshipped — and not dress.

When that day brought sweet rest and peace,

Not glitt'ring show — voluptuous ease !

Prompt as the bells' loud, noisy beat,

We took our long accustomed seat ;

List'ning, not for accents clear,

Reasoning, logic, nor to hear

The flights of florid eloquence

Of modern days ; but recompense

That God will truly, surely give

To those who work, and toil, and strive ;

The thirsty pilgrim nears the fount,

But does he stop the odds to count

Between the rustic cup or spring,

And goblets flashing jeweling ?

And thus the thirsty, parched soul

Drank the pure waters of the Word:

Good as they came from God's own hand:

Listened, and welcome promise heard.

Again the long week ushered in

Its Monday morn: through the light, thin

Fog that laid along the rough bank

Of trees and hills, and, feasting, drank

The first bright rays of morning dawn,

Hiding from view the meadow lawn,

How many eager, watching eyes

Sought weather-omens in the skies!

And, with prescient knowledge, told

O'er the old quaint rhymes, to unfold

The secrets of the coming day.

And — when driving the mists away

With one wild foray of his bright,

Heav'n-lighted darts, and with the might

Of his kingly presence, sweeping

Down into the valleys, — creeping

Through shadowed, night-like gorge and glen,

And overturning in the fen

The night-attendants gathered there !

   Laughing to the dew-weighed flower,

Making its petals glitter fair

   With wondrous charm and magic power,

Uprose the sun — our hearts throbbed free,

With wild and glad expectancy !

For this, our long-planned gala-day,

Had promise of rare rustic glee.

Ere long, we gathered on the green,

With happy faces ; not the mean

And studied smile which Art bestows

   On deep and scheming Flattery,

But the rich, warm, meaning glows

Bequeathed each Nature's devotee:

With all their trappings and their show,
Prancing horses, proud drivers, now
Swept down the merry cavalcade, —
Past gates and bars, soon to be made
Proud portals, for the golden grain
　To pass triumphant! swiftly by
Farm-houses, with their marks of gain,
　And rustic joy and revelry.
Sped over swiftly bounding brooks;
Saw shapes in grim and haunted nooks;
Caught the long branches drooping low
From limbs, that wildly seemed to throw
Their great, cool arms across the way,
And wish us all "a happy day"!

At last we reached our pic-nic ground;

WINTER-FREED.

A mossy bank, rich sloping down
To greet the ripples of the lake,
Which kiss its edge, and oft awake
Low, murmuring music, like the rise
And fall of feet in Paradise !
A little spot, low nestling down
    Between the hills, as a fear-made
Child, fearful of the shadows thrown,
    Sinks 'neath the drap'ry overlaid.
Great trees, whose branches far outswing,
And interchange grave nods, and bring
A thousand thoughts and legends told
Of wild-wood feasts, and Druids old, —
Their richest foliage gladly fling
To form a leafy covering.

Some wander through the deep old woods, —
    Climb ledges, thick with wild vines grown,

Seek dark, low caves, where echoes back

   The voice, in low, sepulchral tone!

Or search some low and sandy beach;

Where the vexed waves and bright sun bleach

The smooth-worn stone, and turn them o'er,

Seeking the shells, to hear their roar,

And dream of Ocean's raging shore!

Others the loaded baskets guard,

And spread upon the velvet sward

Our sylvan feast, teeming with fare

Such as a king might wish to share.

And now announced, we hungry come,

And, seated, join the noisy hum;

Pass comments on each high-piled dish,

   Accept, with rustic chivalry,

The cup of water, from the spring

   That bubbles just across the way

From rustic waiting-maids; with eyes
Pure as Pleiads in the skies;
And shining curls bright as the sun —
Which struggling with the mists, has won
The mountain's top, to gild its sides —
Sends his burnished gleams, and glides
Like fairy spirits o'er lone hearts,
The foliage down — tints all its parts,
And tips the leaves with light like gold —
Accept the cup — a moment hold —
Survey the liquid, diamond-clear;
Then quaff, and swear it pearly tears,
Or nectar, from a hand more fair
Than Hebe's, whose labor was to bear
The drinking-cups to gods of myth!

And thus, in quick succession, went
Bright, joyous scenes of merriment:

WINTER-FREED.

With mingled jokes, and oddities

Experienced all pic-nic days ;

Until the sunbeams, faint and few,

In seeming reluctance, withdrew

To swell the western sea of fire,

And watch their sun-god's slow retire :

While we, full gorged with happiness,

Longed for our homes and sleep's caress —

Glad as at morn, retraced our way.

Just as the birth and launch away

Of all fond hopes : they fade and blight,

Or, smothered in their gathered might

Of richness full — each — all that went

Return when the long day is spent,

To lay them down in some warm part,

And throbbing corner of the heart,

To find new solace for the pain,

Or rest, and gather strength again !

WINTER-FREED.

When next the light, grey dawn appears,

And the Eastern Shepherd, through tears

Down-weighing flower, and trees, and grass,

As barriers for his train to pass

In magisterial sway, brings

His gifts and golden offerings,

Our clustered valley homes to light —

Far as extends the peering sight,

Out past the wood-lot's long extent,

And circling round the river's bent,

And everywhere resounds again

The reapers' voices in the grain !

Yes, rich and laden harvest-time,

With gathering sheaves, and tinkling rhythm

Of sharp'ning sickles, and the drawn

Loads, waiting at the gate-post tall

For mischief-makers springing on,

And, with their rides, delaying all.

Summer's past; and through sighing trees,

Spirits and mourning sprites, and leaves,

Of mellow brown and russet gold,

With flittings swift, dominion hold.

The high clambering ivy vine

Hugs closer to the tree, and twines

Its little tendrils around arm

And branch, to guard them from the storm.

The air is soft and dreamy still,

And gauze-like, silken fibres fill

And gleam along the autumn sky:

And, flitting slowly, shadows lie

Like shades upon a picture there

Along the valley; everywhere

Low hangs the light, dream-giving smoke;

And, as a dying man, awoke

Before the last, deep, fearful strife,

Views the trembling balance of life,

And, in the silence, utters prayer,

So, still and pulseless seems the air.

Corn-husking o'er; fruits gathered in;

   The winter's wood all weather-fast:

We wait its snow-winged heralding

   Prepared to meet its raging blast!

Waft, Angel of these later days!

Thy silken drift and dreamy haze:

Touch, with the magic of thy wand,

And seal more close the gathering bond

That binds us to the spirit-land!

Reach out thy soft and tender hand,

And, as the little child, which wakes

From its deep sleep, and hostage takes

WINTER-FREED.

Of the bright pleasures of the morn,

Still pleasures though in sadness born,

And smiles, and sinks away again,

Rememb'ring not the day's least pain,

So guide us o'er the shores which meet;

With happy visions, quick to greet

Us, coming from our youthful days

To wake, and in the deepening maze

Of dreams, to give us joy, and flame

Such lighted smiles o'er weary frames

As almost gleam from angel-eyes,

Lit with the gold of Paradise!

www.ingramcontent.com/pod-product-compliance
Lightning Source LLC
Chambersburg PA
CBHW021438090426
42739CB00009B/1533